796.7   Barrett, Norman S.
Bar   Trailbikes

DATE DUE   PERMA-BOUND

796.7   Barrett, Norman S.
Bar   Trailbikes

PICTURE LIBRARY

TRAILBIKES

TRAILBIKES

Norman Barrett

Franklin Watts

London   New York   Sydney   Toronto

First Paperback Edition 1990
ISBN 0-531-15173-5

© 1987 Franklin Watts Ltd

First published in Great Britain
     1987 by
Franklin Watts Ltd
12a Golden Square
London W1R 4BA

First published in the USA by
Franklin Watts Inc
387 Park Avenue South
New York
N.Y. 10016

First published in Australia by
Franklin Watts
14 Mars Road
Lane Cove
2066 NSW

UK ISBN: 0 86313 492 0
US ISBN: 0-531-10277-7
Library of Congress Catalog Card
Number 86-50643

Printed in Italy

Designed by
Barrett & Willard

Photographs by
Action Plus

Illustration by
Rhoda & Robert Burns

Technical Consultant
Richard Francis

Contents

Introduction

There are many exciting motorcycle sports that take place off the road or track. The motorcycles, or trailbikes, used in off-road sports are built for rough treatment.

They have thick knobby tires for gripping loose surfaces, and strong shock absorbers and springs to smooth out the jolts and bumps.

△ Motocross is one of the most popular of the off-road motorcycle sports. Competitors race around several laps of a difficult cross-country course.

Motocross is a popular off-road sport. It involves racing over a rough cross-country course. Supercross is similar, but is held inside a stadium, with obstacles.

In trials riding, balance and skill over very rugged terrain are more important than speed. Enduros, in which riders must keep to strict time schedules, are tough endurance tests for both bike and rider.

△ In trials, there are special sections designed to test riding skills. A rider must have complete mastery over the bike to avoid penalty points.

The off-road bike

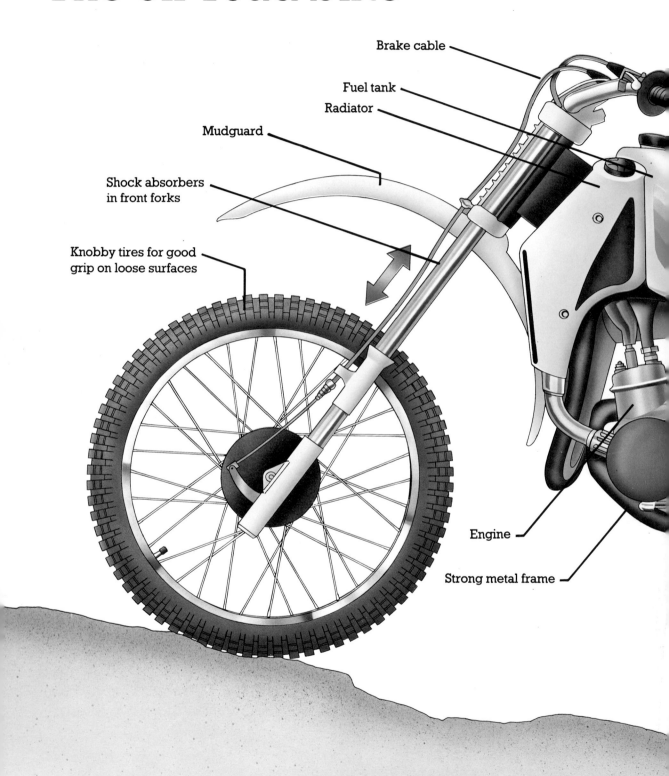

Brake cable

Fuel tank

Radiator

Mudguard

Shock absorbers
in front forks

Knobby tires for good
grip on loose surfaces

Engine

Strong metal frame

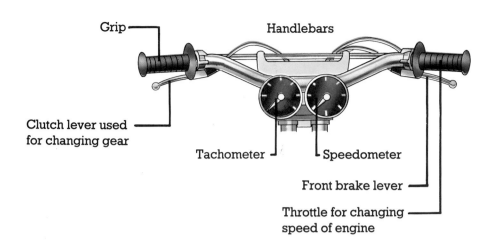

Grip

Handlebars

Clutch lever used
for changing gear

Tachometer

Speedometer

Front brake lever

Throttle for changing
speed of engine

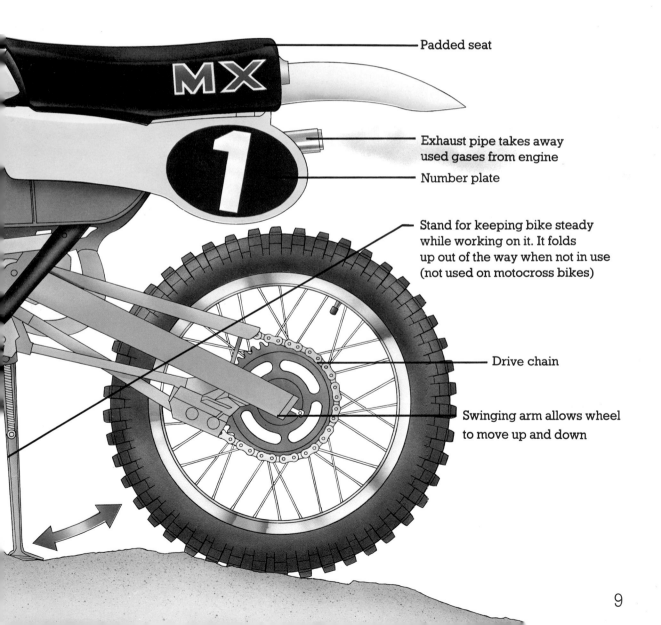

Padded seat

Exhaust pipe takes away
used gases from engine

Number plate

Stand for keeping bike steady
while working on it. It folds
up out of the way when not in use
(not used on motocross bikes)

Drive chain

Swinging arm allows wheel
to move up and down

Motocross

For motocross, or scrambling, as it is sometimes called, the course is marked out on rough, hilly ground.

The bikes are light but strong. Riders have to maneuver them around sharp bends and up and down steep slopes on all kinds of loose and hard surfaces.

Riders wear protective clothing, including helmets, face masks, padding and strong boots.

△ The riders line up for the start of a motocross race. As soon as the starting gate goes up, the bikes roar into action. The course soon narrows, so the riders who start first gain a clear advantage.

▷ A rider takes off from a steep slope. Great skill is needed to control the bike when landing on a loose surface.

▽ As a race proceeds, the riders tend to spread out along the course. But one slight mistake and a rider can be easily overtaken.

▷ A bunch of riders jostle for position as they scramble up a steep hill.

It is easy to see why protective clothing and face masks are so important, as the bikes throw up loose stones and dirt into the faces of the following riders.

Motocross is a highly organized sport. There are international competitions and world championships. The top riders are sponsored by bike manufacturers and can earn big prize money.

Championships are held for different classes of bikes. As many as 40 riders might take part in a race. There are also special events for young riders.

△ Instructions or information are held up for a rider by a member of his team. At the top level, motocross is a joint effort, with mechanics backing up the riders.

A typical motocross course winds up and down and around for about 1¼ miles (2 km). Races may be held over 20 laps or more.

On the faster parts of the course and downhill, the more powerful bikes reach speeds of over 70 mph (110 km/h). But because of the difficulty of the course, the average speed is more likely to be about 30 mph (50 km/h).

△ The checkered flag signals the end of the race, and hundreds of spectators cheer the winner of a big international event.

Supercross

A particularly popular form of motocross is called supercross. This is held in a stadium over an artificial course built up from sand and other materials.

Spectators can watch all the action while sitting in comfort, without having to climb up muddy banks and through woods to reach the best viewing points.

△ A packed stadium enjoy the thrills of supercross. Two riders struggle to control their machines as they fly together through the air.

▷ Negotiating mounds of loose dirt on a supercross circuit can be more difficult than on a natural outdoor course.

16

Trials

In motorcycle trials, riders have to negotiate tricky natural obstacles without stopping or putting a foot on the ground.

Trials are held over distances ranging from a few miles to the six-day events over as much as 1,000 miles (1,600 km). There are also indoor events called arena trials.

▽ Rocks, mud, tree roots and even overhanging branches are hazards that face the trials rider. The bikes are equipped with special engines and gears that enable the rider to move very slowly without stalling.

The obstacles on a trials course are called "sections." They might vary in length from 22 to 330 yd (20 to 300 m). Sections include such hazards as large boulders, loose rocks, deep mud, fast-flowing water, steep climbs and sharp turns.

Riders lose one penalty point for "dabbing," or putting a foot down, and five for stopping. Between sections, they may rest or work on their bikes.

△ A turbulent stream proves too much for one rider, whose bike has broken down. Once he stops, he receives the maximum penalty of 5 points for the section.

◁ A rider tackles a slippery section high up in the Scottish mountains. The Scottish Six-Day Trial is one of the leading international events.

Only one rider at a time is allowed on a section. Riders have a chance to inspect each section before they ride through it. They are often able to see how other competitors fare, so they can plan their own tactics on the section.

There are observers on each section to mark penalty points, or award a "clean" if a rider completes the section without penalty.

Enduro

Enduros are long-distance events over rough country. Riders set out at intervals and are timed over each stage. They try to get from one checkpoint to another in a set time.

An enduro is also a test of reliability. The bikes are modified motocross machines. No major replacement is allowed during the race and the riders have to do their own repairs.

△ An enduro rider wears protective clothing even in the heat of the desert. He also needs to carry provisions and the necessary tools and small parts to carry out running repairs.

▷ All kinds of terrain
are covered in enduros,
including coastal
stretches as well as
deserts.

▽ A stop for tire repairs
on the Paris-Dakar rally.
This runs from France
to the west coast of
Africa and lasts nearly
three weeks. Other
famous enduros include
the International Six-
Day Enduro, which is a
world championship
team event, and the Baja
1000 in Mexico.

Other off-road sports

△ Grass-track racing takes place on grass circuits about 350 yd (320 m) round. With eight riders to a race, the top grass is soon worn off.

▷ Drifting around bends is tough on both rider and bike.

△ Arena trials take place indoors or inside a stadium. They are like trials riding, but with artificial sections, or obstacles.

◁ A section in arena trials – riding over a car!

25

△ Sand, or beach, races are a popular form of off-road sport. Bikes compete with three-wheel all-terrain vehicles. Normally, they all race in the same direction, but bumpy sand dunes sometimes turn vehicles around!

◁ A sidecar combination competing in a beach race.

There are special events for all-terrain vehicles (ATVs), usually with three, but sometimes with four, wheels. These balloon-tire vehicles can operate on all kinds of surfaces, as the name suggests.

▷ A rider gets airborne while negotiating a jump.

▽ Grasstrack racing on ATVs.

The story of trailbikes

The first trials

Motorcycles have been used off the beaten track even since they were invented. In the early days of this century, they were the best means of traveling in forested areas.

Trials riding started in England. It developed from the pastime of riding road bikes through woods and open country. Riders began to race against each other and to test their riding skills. Trials were soon organized and as the sport grew popular they became longer. The first International Six-Day Trial, an enduro event, was held in England in 1913.

△ Supercross, a stadium version of motocross popular in the United States.

△ The sidecar passengers are not getting an easy ride in this very muddy trial.

A rare old scramble

In 1924 in the south of England, a group of riders decided to stage a new version of trials – without the observed sections. It turned out to be a race over the roughest ground possible, and one of the officials said it was a "rare old scramble." That is how scrambling got its name, and it was not until much later that it came to be known as motocross.

This first scramble was held in Surrey and fewer than half the original 80 entrants finished the course. No one was hurt, though, and the event proved to be a huge success. At the end, the course was littered with headlamps, exhaust pipes and any other accessories the riders could shed to give their machines more maneuverability. Right up to World War II (1939–45), competitors rode their bikes to the races. It was not until after the war that specialized machines were developed.

△ A youth class grasstrack race.

Spread of the sport

Off-road motorcycling grew in popularity after the war. World championships were staged for both motocross and trials riding. The sport spread from Europe to the United States, where supercross was born.

Motocross and grasstrack racing now have events for young riders, boys and girls of six years and upwards.

△ Australian trials rider Beverley Anderson. Women compete with men on equal terms.

Women have taken part in trials since the early days. They compete on equal terms with the men and some have achieved considerable success.

There are classes for sidecars in both scrambling and trials. The latest development in off-road machines, the all-terrain vehicle, is becoming increasingly popular around the world.

△ Three-wheel all-terrain vehicles in action.

Facts and records

World championships

The first Motocross World Championships were held in 1957. There are classes for 500cc, 250cc and 125cc bikes, and for sidecars. Riders earn points towards the world title in 12 races, or grands prix, staged in different countries.

There has been a World Trials Championship since 1975. Trials counting toward the title are mostly one-day events, over a

△ Riding an observed section in a world championship trials event.

course of about 30 miles (50 km), with up to 40 observed sections.

Long-distance events

The longest off-road races are the six-day trials and the enduros. The Scottish Six-Day Enduro is held over about 1,000 miles (1,600 km), the same distance as the Baja 1000 enduro, in Mexico. Some enduros are even longer. The International Six-Day Trial, the world championship of enduro racing, is almost twice as long, and riders in the Paris-Dakar rally cover as much as 6,2000 miles (10,000 km).

△ A rider on a 500cc machine competing in a motocross grand prix.

Glossary

All-terrain vehicle (ATV)
A small motorized vehicle with three or four balloon tires raced on all kinds of soft, loose and bumpy surfaces.

Arena trials
Trials held in a stadium or an enclosed area, with obstacles.

Clean
A section of a trial completed without penalty.

Dabbing
Putting a foot down in a section of a trial. The penalty is one point for each dab up to a maximum of three in any section.

Enduro
A long-distance race over rough country decided on time.

Grand prix
A race that counts toward the World Championship in motocross.

Motocross
Race over cross-country course.

Section
An observed part of a trial that competitors must ride over without putting a foot down or stopping. Penalties incurred in each section are added up to produce the riders' final scores. The rider with the fewest penalty points wins the trial.

Shock absorbers
Devices on a bike that cushion the jolts and make the ride smoother.

Sidecar
A small carriage with its own wheel, attached to a bike or built as part of it, for carrying a passenger. There are special classes in motocross and trials for sidecar machines.

Speedometer
Dial showing speed of bike.

Supercross
A form of motocross held in stadiums with artificial obstacles.

Tachometer
Dial showing speed of the engine in revolutions per minute.

Trial
A cross-country sport in which competitors must ride over special sections without stopping or putting a foot down. It is often called the "feet-up sport."

Index